INTO THE FIRE

Forward

I am certainly not the first person to be awed by the way poetry can universalize emotions and give voice to what we, the human race, share about our experience. Poetry has such a peculiar capacity to transcend the pettiness of our thoughts and opinions and those trivial differences, the importance of which is the product of acculturation or the unresolved charge we have on the painful moments of our lives.

After reading this collection of poems, I was struck by the mysterious way in which a good poem strikes a chord in the psyche and brings the gift of understanding to a certain feeling. By what means does it call up our personal experience in such a transpersonal way? I cannot explain it. I can only feel its effects.

Good poems are offered up in an endless variety of forms. There are those that sweeten our mood. Others that conjure spectral emotions from the stories we have woven around the events of our lives. There are those that startle us and humor us. And there are those that catalyze a process which leads to greater clarity about a memory, once vague or poorly understood.

It is a rare privilege to witness a creative process as it is conceived, birthed and honed into its final form. It is even more rare to know a poet and know something about the circumstances that provided the raw materials for the artistic self-expression crafted from words and the deepest of feelings.

The poet, in this case, happens to be my friend. We have shared experiences, shared our process, witnessed enough moments of each other's lives to have developed an experiential short-hand in the way we can recall what we have learned about each other. And we continue to accumulate rich stories about times we have spent in each other's company. When I stumble upon a line in one of Meg's poems which clearly refers to me, it never fails to send a pleasant shock wave through me. However, this pales in comparison to that moment when an event in her life (about which I may happen to know) appears, as if by magic, as a collection of carefully chosen words which, together in a certain order, illuminate something quite invisible in the ordinary sense, and that is her emotional response to what life brings her.

I hope you will savor this collection as much as I do. May the words delight and provoke you. May they touch you deeply and profoundly. I know Meg, so I can say without equivocation that you are being granted one of those uncommon opportunities to see deeply into a very open heart. May it serve to grow and open your own.

-Jennie Marlow
Teacher, Speaker, Author

Words Collected on the Road to Silence

INTO THE FIRE

MARGARET COYLE IRSAY

Welcome

This collection of words and images represent the continuing story of my life unfolding. I have collected them and gathered them here in order to give face and voice to the story of my heart's opening. These poems breathe and heave, bend and sway to give sound and shape to the story of my awakening, to the story of my journey up the river of differentiation in the name of authentic being. They are my perspective and they sing from the recognition and acceptance that even though life is full of uncertainty it is possible to live this fact with curiosity, faith, compassion and dignity. This book is a living artifact of my intention to be, and to be in community. May it touch your heart and open your eyes to a clearer vision for reconciling the fear of life's uncertainty and may that vision light the path for you to follow toward a deeper understanding of what it means to live with balance.

May you find comfort and encouragement within

- Meg Coyle Irsay

INDEX

11. Cooking the Questions

12. Community of Me
    12. Need
    14. Intention
    17. Surrender
    18. Humility
    20. Questions
    23. Practice
    25. Relationship
    26. Balance
    29. Service
    30. Faith

32. Vision of the Heart
36. Oh My Life
38. My Yoga is on the Move
43. Love Flow Poem
46. The Illusion is
50. Now Listen Here
54. Closer Look
58. Fit To Judge
60. Border Town
62. Have You Lost Weight?
63. Learning to Breathe
64. It Takes Time
66. My (Experience of) Wisdom
67. Spontaneity
68. Again and Again
71. The Light Has Come
72. Easter Time
74. This is Living
78. Surfs Up
81. Qigong
83. Oh, My Kinfolk
84. Sick of Me
89. Don't Forget

Cooking The Questions

Cooking the questions
down to the bone
with a heart to travel
all the way home.

Throw every thing
you think you know
into the fire
and watch now
how authentic choice
exposes true desire.

Community of Me

Need

I need to hear the stories
the stories of coming to Truth.
I want to learn of coming to
and going all the way through
every lie ever told
the misconceptions that I hold
every habit born of fear
these attachments I hold dear.

I feel my story as yours is told
and I'm grateful for a hand to hold.
My conditioned mind persists in its planning
so how can I use it to understand
the facts about what's true for both me and for you?

Through your tales of trial and error
I find real comfort for the terror
of surrendering my grip on fantasy
and coming at last to a lasting peace.

With your stories and my best plan
like Dumbo on high, feather in hand
I'm able to test what I think that I know
as I dive into the whelming mystery below.

With your support and a gust of courage
I dive into what is yet unheard of.
I move into what I have not yet seen
navigating the dark corners of what I believe.
Feeling the feather of support in my hand
I find strength to trust in a much broader plan.

With your presence and your good company
I find new access to the capacity
to trust that my increasing faith in essence
is dismantling my impulses to resort to defenses.

Your honesty is what teaches me
to learn to trust this mystery
through what has taught you to learn to see,
remember and accept the truth of your freedom.

Intention

The parts of me torn asunder
long this day to feel the wonder
of living with loving, faithful intention
free from the fear of my mind's intervention.

The part of me that boldly goes
where fear warns no woman has gone before
travels the vastness of the void
forgetting the fear that has kept me avoiding.

The parts of me that are locked in defense
can't see how forgiveness can make any sense.
While the heart of me that knows to trust
feels the drag of fear and rust
and trusts despite my fear of living
trusts that I can find clear vision.
This part of me that somehow knows
is cleaning the closet of what my mind holds.

What will survive these shifts of mind?
What will be saved what will be left behind
when I find the faith to trust and release
my fantasies in the name of my peace?

Surrender

I consider my thinking and I think that if I
want to know how to live then my hopes have to die.
If I truly want truth to pervade in my life
I will need to be honest about what I am fighting.

The freedom to accept a viable solution
that will reconcile fear with love's evolution
arrives through acceptance that the truth of the whole
is composed of One Love expressed as each soul.

And the means to stand under and embrace this truth
is not often so easy.
There are trials as well as errors all along the road to dignity.

The ones who are genuinely walking this road
and meeting the risks and the challenges it holds
have learned that the way is not to seek refuge
but instead to find courage in the face of the deluge
of forces that are only seeming to oppose them.

Surrendering the desperate and futile hunt
for a life where there's no more trouble to run from
is the place where the journey of living begins
moving through the pain
to the quiet within.

Humility

To gain an understanding of my dis-ease
I have to be willing to look and to see
where I am now in this moment presenting
starting out broadly then narrowing in.

Lensing in and lensing out
with careful attention I can recognize doubt
and see it split truth into opposing opinions
fueled by what I imagine to be outside Love's dominion.

Finding the willingness to question these doubts
enables new perspective to take seed and sprout.
I take in what Love reminds me I know
and plant it with patience and tend to its growth.

Through careful intention and dedicated practice
I can answer the moment with renewed capacity
to question beyond my present perspective
allowing my mind to work more objectively.

Questions

What are my patterns of fear and delusion?
What are the seeds buried deep in confusion?
What and where am I spending the life force
that supplies my life's essence and connection to Source?

In my endeavor to increase understanding
I humbly stand in the place where I am
and consider everything I believe that I know
looking for relationship back to the whole
forth to my single and absolute goal
of understanding and peace of mind.

I feel the bones of my thinking
and the muscles of my actions
collaborating to form
the body of my experience.
I look to the shifts
I can see now must happen
for my mind to be calm
in this process
of awakening.

Practice

What my fearful mind would call a problem
my patient heart calls a lesson
and every lesson teaches the same solution
to every imagined problem through forgiveness.

The capacity to surrender *what I have thought to be*
for the vision forgiveness wants to show me
is my single, primary, objective aim.
Forgiveness is transporting me out of the shame
that has captured and held my love of living in chains.

The growing capacity to see through the old
all the way to the new in the light of this day
is the miracle of forgiveness.

Relationship

When relationship has been confused with guilty obligations
when community has been inundated with fearful expectations
the challenge to feel our collective intention to see each other without
shame's intervention can only be answered by cultivating the ways
to suspend our reactions to what our fears say.

So how do we feel the community we need through the smoke of reaction to the fear Love could leave us? How do we learn to practice trust in the face of the fear that we could somehow be excluded from Grace? What is correct to choose in the name of understanding ourselves instead of assigning blame?

The future is uncertain. This can be seen as the basis for living a life of humility or the justification for believing we are doomed to surviving the ill-fated destiny of trying to survive a cruel God's vengeance.

Practicing the willingness to investigate outside of what we presume to be fate opens us up to the ways we can learn that with disciplined practice our reality can turn back toward the peace we can feel our hearts calling from.

Learning to trust what we think we don't know with the persistence of one who wants most to know growth yields a certain confidence in accepting uncertainty as a real point of balance. And learning to trust and surrender our thinking into the hands of a life of uncertainty will take every bit of humility we can muster.

I am reminded that if I am not seeing perfection in what is presenting itself in this moment both in my sorrows as well as my joy then I am not yet seeing.

And so I look and look again, forgiving my mind for its misinterpretations. I breathe and allow my mind to be cleared of resentment through the earnest and patient practice of forgiveness.

Balance

When we manage to accept the means to grow
out of the holes of feeling loveless and lonely
we transform according to love's evolution.
And we must find the ways to stand ready and brave
as we meet our resistance to releasing behavior
that is clearly not serving our deepest intention
to know God and show God in our words and our actions.

I dig into the places marked by my fears using my sturdiest questions. *What will the nature of my family be when I arrive at the acceptance of reality? Of the ones I am calling my kin today which of these if any are kin to the circumstances of my deepest truth and purpose?*

The course our questions set send us out to navigate the frontier between our biology and our psychology, between our personal experience and the collective One, between our ancestors and our descendants. Our questions are the boat that hold us in the current of spirit moving the infinite diversity of existence with a single intention to awaken.

Standing on the crest of time with a stiff wind blowing in my face I open my chest, take in a full breath and shake and shake and shake in agreement with all that is present for the whole human race. I take It All in and I let the breath go as I wait for response from what my heart knows.

Service

So what can be said about any of It in a way that would tell the real story of the relationship between what we call heaven on earth and what we call living a hell? The words alone are words alone so how do they come to ring with the essential meaning for you and for me in a voice we're both able to hear?

How do the words we find ourselves using come to ring with real truth and real meaning? The best that I can say today is that when the words I speak are not orphans but are parented by my plain and honest response to what I am feeling in present time, they are able to ring with the truth.

When the words I speak are totally embodied they speak for the holy whole of humanity. When the words and actions taken and given are calm and confident regardless of the particular company they find themselves in, or the circumstance they arrive into, or the form they use to communicate they will become the living song of the Truth.

Words and actions that are faithful to an authentic response will demonstrate faith. And faith is the means to navigate uncertainty. When we can stand on the board of compassion and balance the water with the wind and pulse of all of existence, along with our imaginations, our emotions, and the inspiration of the unknown, the combined dance will speak to and from our absolute Unity.

This capacity is very good news.

Faith

I see you and I study what I see.
I hear you and I hear you name me.
I feel you and I feel the need
to allow freedom to teach us the fact that we're free.
I see
and I hear
and I feel
and I am studying
and considering responsiveness
before I do anything.
So what can this litany of words be about?
What can I say in response to my doubts?
God if I know and I know if I panic my fears will find food to feed reasons to panic. So what can I say except to say this- that practicing to learn well the ways to stay calm when the truth hits the shit of my managed aplomb is the whole and the reason of why I'm alive. I accept that in growth the old has to die.

I accept there is always some kind of a bomb to bust the new out of the old and carry on with the unpredictable story of creation now unfolding.

So, hey, hey, what can I say after the bomb has been dropped?
Nothing if I'm living instead of surviving, nothing if I accept I can't stop it. So I'll close my mouth and open my mind as well as my ears and listen behind and under every word I hear for the sound of the spirit washing my fears. And each time I find the faith to wait and trust I have courage to help me remain trusting of what is now presently happening, I find *I am* the way to walk through each explosion while learning to face fear without blowing big holes in the dignity of my divinity.

Vision of the Heart

I am going
and I am gone
and I am here
and I am now
setting my sail
to heave and to leave what I have believed to be true
to set and set sail on the wind and a prayer
for the hidden and beckoning
reaches of The Heart.

I can hardly bear to go
and I can no longer bear to go on
without the certainty of who I Am.

I can hardly bear to go
and I can no longer bear to go on
as any thing other than what certainty has named Me.

My sadness is now
and it's perfectly ripe.
I spend all my courage and take a big bite.
And as I taste this now and hear
the story of a foregone fear
I feel my heart aching.
I hear my heart beating.
I feel my resistance buckling and breaking.
I hear my heart sing.
I feel my mind change.
I see how forgiveness transforms and arranges.
I see all the love in this moment resounding.
I feel all these feelings come loose and unwind now.
I look to see what I once held as corrupt
lifting its uncertain chin to look up
and into the face of the Heart with new Trust

that it can now in fact breathe with unanimous love
by remembering the dance of the spirit is innocence
and this dance welcomes everything into magnificence.

Now and with the breath my feelings rise and fall.
Now and with the breath my response is standing tall.

I would give
I do give now
my life, my limb and the sweat of my brow
for the chance to feel the strength of Peace
for the acceptance and the confidence
to trust in a life lived absolutely
from the Truth of My Heart.

My longing for The Truth
is the most genuine thought I hold.
My longing for The Truth
sorts through every thing I know.
It sorts and searches constantly
for the plainest way to practice embodying
the complete acceptance of my Heart's vision
and the means it provides to make better decisions.

I hear the Sea now whispering to me.
I feel the way calling now and moving my feet.
And every river that winds and eventually runs
without hesitation will eventually come home to the Sea.

And the Sea welcomes each and every river that arrives.
And the Sea releases every fluid drop of Love up and to the sky.
And the Sea is you.
And the Sea is me.
And the Sea is both of us at the same time.
You and I are the Sea of We.

This is the heart of what I see.

OH MY LIFE

I've been waiting all my life. I've been waiting to find my way home.
Except, I have not exactly waited
its more like I have run
and hidden
and circled
and done
just about everything but wait.

I've tried to take control.
I've tried to take the blame.
I've tried to take the wheel
when I was clearly in no shape to be driving.

I have been waiting to come. I've been too afraid to go.
I have been waiting for these buses that never seem to show.
I try and wait and wait to try
and while I think I'm waiting I
fold my arms and hold my tongue
and hope for ways to keep me from
the impatience that would have me run
from the lessons that are standing right in front of me.

All my life I've been yearning
like a child in search of her mother
like a mother in search of her daughter
like a fish in search of some water.

I've wandered and wondered and pondered and blundered
out here on my own for too long. I am tired now of carrying the advice
that says life is easier if I remain on my own. After years of fears and
many tears I am sincerely hoping that I am now tired enough.

The only thing left at this stage of the game
is to learn to surrender and trust.

Oh my Life.

I've been waiting.
I've been waiting to know how to wait.

The stillness
has been with me all along.
The stillness
is now my arrival.

My Yoga is on the Move

My yoga is on the move
My yoga is calling me forward
backward and forward and through.

My yoga is turning me inside
and outside and back again.
I am drawn by the hand of my heartbeat right now
to the rhythm of breath and limb.

This blessed thread of Love
that holds me to the truth that I am.
This blessed thread of Love
that turns my soil over again.
This blessed thread of Love
that helps me all ways feel
that even in my pain there lies the truth
if I am willing to see It.

Here I am
on the earth
fallen from Grace
or so it would seem
with two ways to go
or so it would seem.
So how do I know which and what to choose?
How do I learn to stand under what's true?

I listen and wait and pray from my center
collecting the thoughts I hear ringing with wisdom.
All other thoughts must wait and wait
and wait until they're good and ripe
wait until they're steady and calm
wait till they're ready to give up the fight.

And so I wait with All that I am
I aim at God and breathe.
I breathe…
like the mountain that I am.
I breathe…
like the mountaineer that I am
who has imagined and climbed and fallen at times
into dark cluttered corners of what is not mine
spiraling down and into the trials
that have tested my mettle while exposing my pride.

I am the mountaineer
who has wondered with intention
seeking power in Love's witness
seeking power in redemption.

I am the mountaineer
who is climbing these steps-
conviction, *forgiveness*, *gratitude*, and *humility*
on the way to my home in the heart of Peace.

I breathe…
like the mountaineer
who has spent a lifetime
running up this mountain
inch by breathtaking inch
cutting through what just won't move
inch by painful inch
weathering the storms of dieing to be born
inch by transforming inch
climbing and gripping, many times flinching
seeking and searching for some way to see
the clear story of my exile and my recovery.

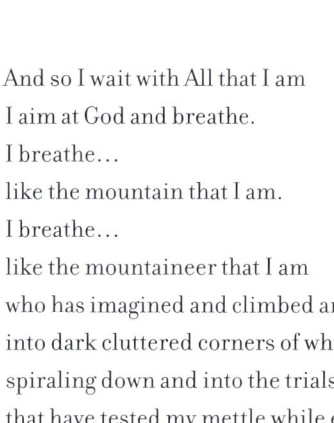

My yoga is pulling me forward
like the sun burning through the mist
like the lover whose heart is leaping in flames
like intention that wants to be kissed.

My yoga is pulling me forward
breathing in me and breathing me out.
My breath is married to living in truth
through my body and my thoughts.

With trust I breathe and notice
what is here and what is now
with trust and a willingness to embrace trail and error
I am understanding more clearly now
how the biology of me meets the psychology of me
where I'm wired by my fears and how this pulls how I steer.

Breathing in I accept the tests
the tests with all the trials
the trials along with their friend error
the seeds that open through fire.
I am understanding more plainly now
Our dance together on earth.
That in trusting Truth I cannot be hurt.
That Love and breath are the engine of life.
That patience and faith will burn through time.
That time can never keep us apart.
That We are truly dancing together.
We are dancing together in time as one Heart.

My yoga sings and I must dance or feel the imagined
fall from Grace. My yoga moves and sings
the true design of my true face.
With my breath and with my words dancing with compassion
I move according to the rhythm of Love
Love and the rhythms of Unity

or I do not move at all
but wait instead to move out of my head
and into the imminent hand of the Truth
that delivers me to the silence.

Home in the heart I feel the start
of creation made in Love's image.
At the center
my mind is home
now
at last
recognized
now
for what it means
to be whole
for what it means
to be holy
for what It is
to be
in truth
in community
with myself and everyone I see
right now.

My yoga is carrying me forward
toward the full memory of my source.
My yoga is carrying me forward
toward the full memory of my Self.
My yoga is carrying me home
toward the knowing that they are One in the same.

Love Flow Poem

I resent it that you could not see me.
I resent you insist that you can.
I resent being taught that my power in this world
could only come by acting more like a man.
I resent it that you could not free me.
I resent you disregard you are free.
I resent you're afraid of your freedom.
I resent that you dominate me.

I don't like it when you box my ears
with your judgments and your unconscious fears.
I don't like the amount of my time
I spend on these problems I know are not mine.

I'm fed up with the promise of what may never come.
I'm fed up with the loneliness of living on the run.
I'm fed up with dis-ease.
I'm fed up with unrest.
I'm fed up with the voice that says I need to be the best.

I hate the world that I was taught through pain and Self-denial.
I hate the lies this world spits out hell bent on mere survival.
I hate it when our wills don't rhyme.
I hate these choices that aren't mine.
I hate that I'm afraid of time.

I'm afraid I'll never find a way to let my mind be still.
I'm afraid my doubts will find some way to trump My Will.
I'm afraid that if I find the trust to live what Love knows
I'll end up here without a friend, homeless and alone.

I'm sorry that I was only a child
dependent on the kindness of strangers.
I'm sorry for the recklessness of disenfranchised anger.
I'm sorry for the ones to whom I've born an untrue witness
forgetting We are born of Love, forgetting Love is sinless.
I'm sorry for my willfulness.
I'm sorry for my pride.
I'm sorry for the vanities that pushed humility aside.
I'm sorry for not acknowledging the Light inside of me.
I'm sorry by not doing that it made Me hard to see.

Please forgive me every form of fearful apprehension.
Please forgive my fearfully driven exaggerated reactions.
Please forgive me for the times I choose retaliation
over simple, timely, compassionate, dignified, honest conversation.
Please forgive me for abandoning my Self to my last hope.
Please forgive me all the things my desperate last hope spoke.
Please forgive the prejudice that kept my heart in jail.
Please forgive my choice to trade my dignity for bail.
Please forgive my tolerance for the ruthless voice of sin
that tells me I have lost my chance to forgive and begin again.
Please forgive the lack of trust that keeps Love on review.
Please forgive me everything that keeps my heart from you.

I didn't mean to let my heart get buried in distrust
I didn't mean to trade mere sight for the vision I *can* trust.
I didn't mean to feed my choice into the hands of drama
by sacrificing what I need for what my fears have wanted.

I want to live without excuse and feel your warm acceptance.
I want to feel the confidence of practicing forgiveness.
I want to come to know myself and give up these illusions.
I want to know you as myself and reconcile confusion.
I want to feel my life belong to what my heart has shown me.
I want to pledge in every form allegiance to this freedom.

I want to love, I want to live the path of liberation
engaging and dancing spirit body and mind in loving transformation.

I understand that what I need is in fact what you need.
I understand despite this fact we won't always agree.
I understand that Love is here and now is when It shows us
salvation's plan to trust and breathe and learn that we can grow up.
I understand by choosing Truth I walk the path less chosen.
I understand to walk this path requires that all emotions
frozen from a fear gripped mind
must now be thawed and owned as mine
must be acknowledged and expressed
released and set free to profess
that feeling and healing these frozen emotions
allows life to flow from the heart of Love's ocean.

I forgive you for the times your fears hijacked your love of life.
I forgive you for the lies you told so you could hide.
I forgive you for the times your doubts
hacked some crazy twisted routes.
I forgive you for the insanities that carried suffering into our house.
I forgive each thing you tried to try and remember that you can fly.

Not that I need a reason but if I did I'd say
I love you because you are Love.
I love you to this day and beyond this day and back and forth.
I love you from the south and to the North and to the East and to the West
and to all the points in between.
I love you because you're Love and Love has always been.
So you and I we're just like Love we do not end or stop or fail.
Our home in Love is innocence.
This vision lights our way.

I love it best when we remember that We are One together
that All is well and Love is true no matter what the weather.

The Illusion Is

The Illusion is that you are some body responsible for suffering some illusion.

Reality is Peace and It is living joyfully and unharmed just behind your illusions. You simply are free.

The illusion is that the best you can do is struggle, fight, run, or concede in a bad dream where to know love you must beg borrow or steal.

The reality is you are as you are all the love you will ever need.

The illusion is that you are held against your will left with only the hope of escaping.

The reality is that you are free to be. There is nothing real that needs to be escaped. There is only thinking waiting to be transformed.

The illusion is you can only share Love through the body.

The reality is the shared mind We are together makes it impossible to be apart from One another.

The illusion is that your life's meaning is found in the imagined status of your circumstance.

The reality is you are merely experiencing the movie of your perceptions projected through the film of your beliefs.

The illusion is that your essential worth must be proven.

The reality is that you are the very source of Love. You are the active ingredient in forgiveness. You are the very love of life.

The illusion is that you could be incomplete.

The reality is that the source of life's potential finds its source in you.

The illusion is that you are insignificant, tired, and weak.

The reality is that you are brother to the planets. You are sister to the oceans. The movement of your breath dances you from the beginning of time to the end joined with every living thing in this absolutely perfect symphony of living.

The illusion is that you must resentfully defend yourself against an endless litany of dangerous attacks.

The reality is that every attack you perceive is coming from inside your own resentments.

The illusion is that this is a poem.

The reality is that this is more then a poem.

This is some fresh air.
This is your best try.
This is the humility to forgive and start over.
This is a fantasy gone by.

This is your empty stomach.
This is an empty stare.
This is what is coming.
This is you'll know when you get there.

This is your aching back.
This is your glass half full.
This is a flat tire on the expressway.
This is you gathering wool.

This is a stranger's smile.
This is resentful denial.
This is a barfing cat.
This is you looking back.

This is a human savior.
This is some human, animal behavior.
This is a permanent substitute teacher.
This is an unidentified creature.

This is your kite stuck up in a tree.
This is your one chance fancy and free.
This is the beginning the beginning of the end.
This is your moment of truth.
This is the fog rolling in.

This is a leap of faith.
This is a dead man walking.
This is love versus hate.
This is apathy stalking.

This is a knee bent at the altar.
This is a prayer that love will not falter.
This is a hopeful suicide attempt.
This is your misinformed best defense.

This is a well thought out misunderstanding.
This is a decaying pile of planning.
This is an imperfect work of art.
This is a masterpiece waiting to start.

This is your very best educated guess.
This is one carefully calculated mess.
This is the first thing that you need to do.
This is the last time that I'm telling you
that I will never stop telling you
the reasons why
you are free
you are well
you will see
time will tell

you are loved
you are Love
your life's important
you're enough
This is the absolute
and final word
including all the words
you've ever heard.

You are as everything
to nothing's open hand
and every
single
thing you are
is right where
love is standing.

Now Listen Here

My husband dear I do declare
that fear has gotten in somewhere.
And as I feel it wear my joints
with its angry bitter points
I feel my muscles pulling tight
to try and manage all the fright
I seem to feel when sensing disapproval.

My father dear it's rather queer
I'm finding my life hard to steer.
It seems my power's gone astray.
How or where it's hard to say?
Perhaps the power for my lunch
was stolen by an angry bunch
of bullies who decided I was disappointing.

Either way and all the same
with fear of dominance falling like rain
there's no way for me to find a way
to see my truth through what you say.
I cannot live this fearful creed.
I've found it's just too hard to breathe.

The pity party's now run dry along with weathered worn out eyes.
The fog of guilt and shame's disguises fade before my heart now rising.
It sows the seeds of what I need through faith in my humility.
The regret is finished. The regret is over. Let's forgive and forget and
surrender the score. I've lost my taste for reasons why we should feel
we to have to lie upon this bed of …

"I promise I will keep you safe from all the men who want to take your
freedom from me".

There's no cause to keep this bed
when we could be laughing and dancing instead
on the floor of faith to the music of trust
in an atmosphere of equanimity.

My mother dear now listen here
you cannot hide like that in fear.
The suffering of your captive will
is spilling over and telling its tale in
every detail of desperate pain
to know and trust your heart again.

Mother dear I want you to know
I wish I could have told you a long time ago
how desperately I need the story of your glory
not the dedicated duty of a woman
who is married to her pain
but is not on speaking terms with it.

Closer Look

You might want to take a closer look.
I am not where you think that you left me
the last time you looked up from the book
of the story you wrote about you and me.

I can see that I'm here in the room with you
but I can't feel your gaze meet mine.
I will always be outside the range of your sight
when you look through a narrowed mind.

But if by chance your mind should ease
and if in fact you want to see me
you will definitely have to turn your head
away from what your sick mind says
and turn toward the vision of innocence instead.
If you do you'll find you may
have some different things to say
like please forgive me for my blindness
my one true wish for us is kindness.

I heard about kindness and about good will
from my parents when I was a girl.
Following the yearning to personally learn
to understand what it is that I heard
is my clearest purpose.
This purpose continues to deliver me
to the exact experiences required
to meet and face the fear I've avoided
to face the pain I've denied.

And I marvel at the grip of the insidious fears
and the resistance that holds the Truth under
the ground of the lies that keep us apart
the ground that pushes Peace under.

The insidious fear that would have me behave
in ways far below Love's dignity
perceives that somehow I've been left behind
abandoned to this ambiguity.
The insidious fear that makes fantasies real
attempts to prove that I'm worth less.
This fear will preside until I decide
I will no longer refuse my own breath.

And there have been some to whom I have poured
my sincere and earnest longing
from deep inside my holy place trusting in my belonging.
And what I'm finding and what I've learned
is that forgiveness in truth cannot be earned.
It turns out *I am the Love I long to know.*
It turns out *I'm safe and sound and forever whole.*
It turns out *I'm well and without real cause*
to fear the truth outside the laws
of what I have been trained to think that I am.
It turns out *this training was mostly a sham.*
It turns out *its impossible for fear to alter*
the Truth of Our source and this fact cannot falter.

God help me accept all the beauty and wear it as my first skin
and not become confused and vain ignoring the beauty within.
God help me forgive mean spiritedness in others and in my self.
God help me to surrender the guilt and the shame that have undermined my health.
God help us when we see instead of love a competition.
God keep our minds free of bad dreams and close to real understanding.
God help us when we find a fight instead of love and joy.
God help us trade this win or loose and all of deception's toys.
God help me see the equality of beauty in everything.
God help us see together all that practicing forgiveness brings.

I find no joy in finding fault in you or anyone.
When we place blame on any head we wear it on our own.
We stand together and fall as One; in Truth we can't be lost.
To know the face of love requires we see all fear has cost us.
To face the cost we need to learn to trust our pain and breathe
and choose again from wisdom through the practice of humility.

I would like to feel you know I've done the best I could and can
I don't claim to be perfect but I do know that I am
born of Love and so I must be perfect as Love is.
The aim of my intention is to consistently remember this.

I don't expect I'll be understood a little if at all
but I will never quit believing that I will
eventually know communion with everything
all the time without end.

So you might want to ponder forgiveness and then take a closer look.
If you look from the truth of your heart you will see I'm the perfect reflection of you.
I may not be where you left me if you're using your opinions to see something other that a friend to the truth, the truth of Unity.

We're here in the room together.
Do you have an interest to see me?
Do you have an interest in being seen?
Do you have any questions for me?
Do you have any interest in sharing some time?
Would you like to share some ideas of mine?
How and to what have we remained blind?
I hold all these questions as I ponder our life.
I study the ways we can invite the light
that can teach us to learn to make accurate choices
and teach us to speak from our unified voices.

After many years and many tears and earnest intention to surrender
my fear and I stand in the quiet of all that is somehow still left standing.
In the quiet where the silence of Zero is so fantastically loud it's deafening,
I watch with my faith as the sounds of my past drift out and to the sea.
Out in the deep wide open
I can feel just one question remain.
It's the only ground I can feel under my feet now.
When I hold it without agenda I can feel my mind growing clearer.
When I listen, the ground of this question whispers its invitation
to move into an authentic inquiry.
It reminds me I have nothing to prove.
It whispers its song to me with my own voice.
It whispers to me that my life is my choice.
It whispers… *Now what?*
Now, this moment now with everything that is happening…
What, *which circumstances, which forms are holding the wind of my answer?*
What are the forms that will teach me to see innocence in every face?
I engage my practice.
I set good intention.
I trust and step onto the back of my question.
Now what?
Hoisting the sale of my intention to know God
to know myself
I cast off
setting sail for the land of my Heart.

Fit to Judge

If you are not at peace you are not certain.
If you are not certain you are only of an opinion.
If you are only of an opinion you are not fit to judge.
If you are not fit to judge you have not accepted
the unified voice within you that is capable of judging.
If you have not accepted the unified Voice within you
you have not accepted Yourself.
If you have not accepted Yourself you cannot be certain.
If you are not certain you cannot be at peace.

You must question your illusions to find the Truth.
You must doubt your opinions to find certainty.
Like Abraham, you must take what you think you cherish the most
climb the mountain and lay it on the altar in willing sacrifice.
Until you place your mind and every thought in it
into the hands of God for translation
into the hands of God for transformation
your illusions will stand in front of the Truth and block it from your view.
With your illusions blocking the Truth you will see no road to travel
out of your dis-ease, no direction to turn out from your confusion.

With your trust in God release what you think you are
and listen as you are re-minded.
Listen and follow the
One who perceives your insanity
and sees beyond it.
Listen and follow
the One
all ways waiting to guide you through.

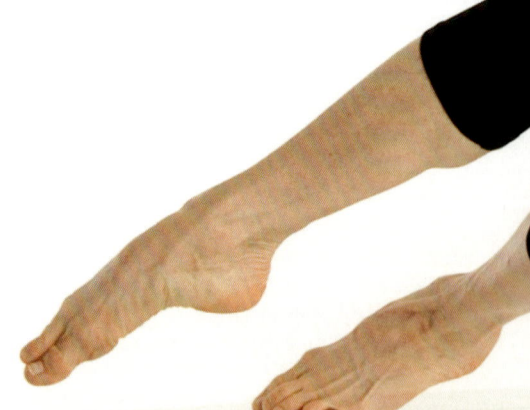

Border Town

Poetry enforces the law of Love
arranging rocks and feathers
in verse that sings the way for saints
and sinners to live together.

Honest living is always edgy.
Honest living is real and messy and sweet.
It's hard to keep the mud off of your boots for too long.

There are phone booths on every corner
for quick changes (of mind)
where street clothes are dropped
revealing capes or wings
or sometimes the agony of the diver
who tries to resist the fall
when her heart
has already left the board.

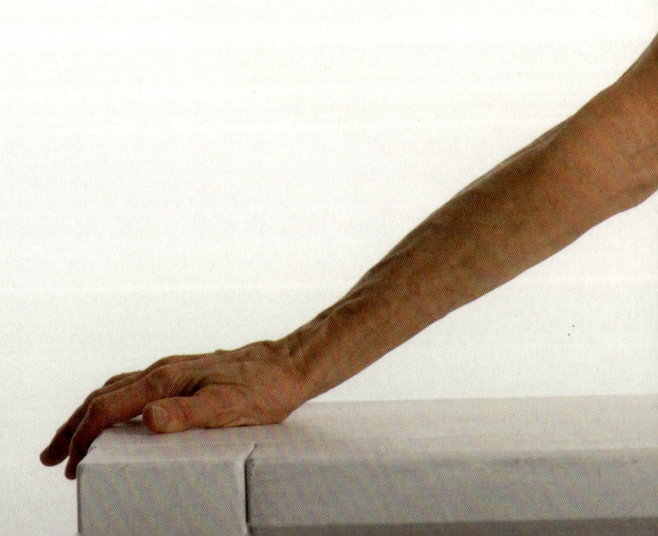

Have You Lost Weight

Have you lost weight or is it your clothes?
Is that a compliment?
It's so hard to know
if when we hear an expression of praise
if the relevance is really about how much we weigh.
Sometimes a compliment can feel a bit bent
if we're not clear ourselves we can't quite tell what's meant
in the swirl of I hope I can manage to be
this or that so I'll somehow be seen as pretty.
And which is the best, to be this or be that
and to do so do I need to be thin or be fat?

Of course what fear sees and what fear can hear
is really a matter of what fear holds dear.
In fear's story of beauty, beauty becomes
the indentured servant of love on the run
bound to the endless exhausting hunt
for a look that will serve as a viable front
for the fear that we must control what we are
making-over our hopes of looking more like the star
of the story we have written right over the truth
that our beauty is real and in all ways absolute.

Understanding our context for hearing a compliment
takes study of that in us needing acknowledgement.
It requires we consider the source of opinion
to learn if that source is love or fear's minion.

So keep in mind that the source of kudos for beauty and class
just may be coming from someone with their head up their ass.

Learning to Breathe

This plan you have for staying calm
won't carry you through you'll need a bomb.
You'll need a crisis and lots of time
to climb up and out of your imagined crimes.

This plan to cover up your scars
cannot release you from your guard.
The path built out of all these sticks
your parents gave you brick by brick
has taken you right up to the wall
but it can't take you through
the opening is too tall.

Your fear of uncertainty has pulled your will tight
and your wild wide heart has been trapped by the fight.
The choice you made to hide behind
the posture of being good and kind
while allowing others to make your decisions
has left you with less than an accurate vision.

What is required to face your fear
and what it has cost will become much more clear
when you come to and accept the fact without worry
that the way you were taught to see is just not working.

The means to understand and realize your calm
can not be made it can only be found.

It Takes Time

Like all relationships it takes time to build and it takes time to dismantle resentment. It takes time to learn just how denial works and it takes time to learn to correct it. It takes what it takes to learn how to learn to see that sight is not vision. Sight is too narrow to hold the whole Truth, too narrow to hold understanding.

Vision provides a perspective that lies in the truth of what is essential with bitterness, anger and frustration to tell us when we are out of integrity.

It is time well spent to learn all we have lent to strategies denying our connection. Plain understanding of restoring real balance is not essentially difficult and consistently practicing the awareness and trust required to build a reconciling fire is not often easy.

Waking up and walking up and out of the shapes of our mistaken thinking is a climb full of sensation. Learning to suspend judgment and wait for a genuine response takes real discipline.

At first, to say the least, it's little awkward. There are stomach aches and heart breaks, and second takes and if you choose to see there are these lucky breaks in the armor of the mind set that keeps us locked in old patterns. When we get out of the way and let forgiveness have say, we make the luck that breaks a clean hole in the bad dream of impossible. The miracle of fresh eyes creates an opening in the misguided and well-practiced fantasy that we could, in any way, at any time, under any circumstances, be disconnected from anything. This clean hole created from freeing old thinking is all that trust requires to locate essential desire and begin the work of allowing new eyes to see through the lies that conditioned tradition has clung to.

Each and one and every time we trust what is and take our time we find the patience to wait and see the actual workings of reality. When we do the sound of our opening heart is the only invitation the garden needs to spring and summer and fall with faith into the winter of our rebirth. When we accept this day and all it has come to say about seeding and feeding and needing together, our garden will grow through what our hearts know in every kind of weather.

My (experience of) Wisdom

My experience of Wisdom arrives through my willingness to wait and respond. My (relationship with) wisdom is the trust I have for the time and space required for accurate formulation and integration of all that I am meeting in real time.

Listening for Wisdom and waiting on wisdom's guidance is my accurate response to what is. My accurate response to what is is the key to my life distinct from survival. Waiting out the impulse to act on my mental decisions is an exercise in patience. Waiting for wisdom to rise and take form in its own time, in its own way, is the exercise of my faith. It is my faith with which I access the truth and my capacity to trust what I am.

By responding instead of deciding I move from trust instead of my fearful reactions. Fear will all ways push me to judge and decide with a deadline. Fear's way is to try and try and take control. From this perspective my life can only be experienced as a competition where loose is always a dreadful possibility. Trust will support me in waiting for discernment and the clear felt response of the knowing within me.

My intellect alone cannot know the essence of what is before me.
Fear cannot recognize the timing of collaboration with the Spirit.
My intellect can only gather information according to sensation.
My intellect does not have the whole and holy story of what is.
My intellect is not the source of my knowing. It is a tool in service of It.

Only my heart can sense and express a true response. Only the breath can hold the knowing that arrives after waiting out every fearful, impatient, conditioned impulse.

This day I choose to slow and feel and see what I can about how I engage with living by breathing and trusting and waiting to respond.

Spontaneity

I am
the balancing point of every opposite
set on the objective wind of infinite possibility.

I am not
a secluded idea impossibly wedged between lifeless options.
no less a vulnerable victim locked down by fearful opinion.

My life on earth can be described
as a collection of events and experiences
relative to the residual context
draped across the face of my essence.
These descriptions of my embodiment's history and ancestry
are what I wear
they are not complete indicators of what I am.
What I am in essence is a much larger story.
What I am in essence is a much clearer glory.

Trying to survive the sensations of resistance to *what is now*
can certainly fill up the days.
And it is only clinging to what has already died that exhausts me.

Spontaneity is the essence of living.
When I am free to live free of fear
living freely fills me.

Again and Again

Sweetness to find you everywhere you are.
These words I am catching
are falling from stars.

It's sweet and it's a sweet relief to be
with each other in community.
Coming and going again and again
coming apart and together to gain
the whole of the story of purpose and action
the holy words given to heal every fraction.

And all along the way I feel the pull and the play of polarity.
Ahhh… the polarity.

I throw myself willingly under the wheels
as they roll me right into the pain to reveal
the cost of my hopes of avoiding the strain
of honestly questioning the roots of these chains
forged of fear's outrage guilt, pity, and shame.

I enter the fire of Love's cleansing alchemy
with no way of knowing what Love will create through me.
I throw myself under the wheels again
like a moth who cannot keep from bashing her brains
into the light of her hearts truest answer
the light that will fill her and feed her and dance her.

It's good to feel you near my friend.
How can I tell you I love you then?
The only way now I can see left to try
is to speak through the silence waiting patiently by.

I am brought to the silence again and again
like an orphan in a world full of big misunderstandings.
And though I may wander and struggle and hide
somehow by Grace I seem to arrive
again to the home I find living inside.
Here inside I find the space
to remember and feel Love's heart-warming embrace.

When It rains it sometimes pours.
My heart is open and it's open to yours.
I make my way toward you to knock on the door
of your sincere intention to understand more
about why and what it is you came here for.

May we awaken to the workings of what can be served
as we learn to live and live to learn
to put down the knife
that pain is a fact
that surviving is not living
that our satisfaction will match our authentic actions
that now is right now and only breath is called for
that now is right now and only breath is fluid enough
to balance the seemingly endless and diverse pieces of our lives
with Grace.

There is a choice to make in every moment.
We can choose to bare our teeth and hold on tight
or we can learn to trust and stay close to the light.

The Light has Come

Its not easy to see the flowers of Peace
in a field of I don't know
that I am the flower as well as the field
in this day of All is well.

The flowers of peace are hard to hold
when my hands are filled with doubt
in the fact that my authentic nature is peace
in the fact that Love is here now.

Its painful to feel the turmoil and death
in a world without forgiveness.
To stand calmly by while my fantasies die
takes great courage, faith and patience.

It's joyful to know I am healed and can heal
by the light that lives within me.
To accept that God's touch creates life through my trust
transforms my world through forgiveness.

It is easy to see with a will that is free
the hand of God moving between Us.
With an open mind and the past left behind
I can see now all that Life offers.

I am grateful to see that come what may
I have all I need in the light of this day.
I am happy to know reap comes straight from sow
and the real truth of living comes from what my heart knows.

Easter Time

After many long nights of tending the tomb
of the life that Love has kept safe for me.
I see now the Son of my heart soon to break
as this dawn shines right through what my guilt sees.
I have waited and paced, and I've worried, and cried
and despite my confusion the light still arrived.

And in the light of the whole story of me
I can see now what Love has determined I see.
I am safe.
All is well.
There's no real cause to fear.
Love will light The Way.
Love will never end.
Love will somehow make this clear.

For the witness of Love rising up from mortality
I thank Jesus and all of the friends who have helped me
to learn that my resistance to Love is unfounded.
It's completely without any true sound or grounding.
I see now nothing real can grow
in the soil of I refuse to know that
I am the Son now on the rise.
Let me receive this Easter Time.

Thank you God for the loving Grace
that teaches me to trust my Holy place.

This is Living

This survival according to opinion
is no thing but an endless race.
These plans aimed at my uncertain future
are an endless, futile, running
from the fear that I have fallen from Grace.
This cannot be called living.
This cannot be my home
a broken down house of ill repute
enslaved to the fear I'm alone.

What would a life look like in which I imagined nothing to fear?
What would a life look like with Essence as my mirror?
What would living be like to balance each color of emotion with the single and
diverse churning of Our collective souls in motion?
What would it feel like to live a life according to the Spirit
the living, holy, loving Spirit living wholly within me?

What can a life hold
one where we accept our commonality
one where we live together gratefully and respectfully
one where we live by the light of our collective need?
What will living mean to us from the perspective of a unified field?
What will our experience be when we choose individually
and together to give up our fearful illusions of sinfulness and separation and
find only Love's kind and patient companions remaining when the work of our
surrender is finished?
What is necessary to learn and to learn to accept our Selves in community
accepting the unearned merits of joy and sharing our absolute Peace?

I can only call this real living.
In this I find my home.
By relinquishing the fear to feel my free Will
I see now it is impossible to be lost.
I see now it is impossible for me to be alone.
If what I imagine to fear is smoke
then what is eternally true is my bones.
My willingness to choose from a will free of fear
builds a structure I can feel and call home.
I let my imagination be fueled by this vision.
I surrender the trespasses of will torn by division
I give all that I can find I believe myself to be
into the hands of This mystery
and I wait.
While I work I wait.
While I rest I wait.
While I wait, I wait for the impulses of Peace
and the responses of my heart
moving from my center
arriving without doubt.
I wait for the pulse that breathes in me
and the very same pulse that breathes out.

My life is fueled by inspiration and through the spirit I see
that thoughts springing from a Mind full of presence
are reminders and encourage me
to move with the essences of what I am.

Time in company with Essence is healing.
Accepting Love's healing presence and evolution is knowing.
Quieting and turning to the center again and again
is the practice that builds trust and confidence
in the Wisdom that guides Us to learn to be wise.

Caring for each other and the earth in one motion
turns the rich soil of our loving devotion to know

with our hearts our Home in each other.
This is Our truth and it is also our weather.

On the ground of truth we find our feet and feel the path of Now.
On the ground with trust our minds relax and feel the way to know.
In the light of knowing we find the strength
to face our fear of uncertainty.
On the road to nowhere we walk together straight into now and here.
Now we move with Heart and Breath.
Now we move with mutual respect.
Now we live without regret.
Now we love with confidence.
Now and forever more we are moved
without the burden of imagined threat.
Now and completely we are moved
by the sway and the sweat of this moment
with nothing to prove
accept that nothing real is in need of proof.
Now we dance together
as the presence of Love
in the face of uncertainty.

Now *this* is what I call living.

Surfs Up

The surf is up
and it's upside down
and it's driving me deep
and down into the ground of my flesh.

The surf is up
and it's upside down
and it's pulling me around
and into what I've imagined would certainly drown me.

The surf it up
and it's upside down
and it's dragging me through
and right up to the lies I've believed I must keep from escaping.

The surf is up
and it's upside down
and it's crashing into all these well thought out plans I've been shaping.

The surf is up
so it must be
time for surfing the waves of me.

It's time and so the time must be now.
It's time to surf so it's time to learn how.

First things first and the first thing I think
is to ride these emotions all the way to the brink
and all the way back again with patience and balance
as this range of emotions is mixed and experienced.
It's time to wait and watch and learn
that new perspective will eventually emerge.

The surf is up
and it's time for testing
the place where I'm standing and the strength of my questions.

Can my questions hold the real weight of the truth?
Can my practice teach forgiveness in a deeply confused world?
Can my present perspective hold the call
to compassionately practice forgiveness above all?
If the answer is no then it's simply too small.

To find a perspective that can hold it All
I can't afford reactions to the fear I might fall.
To balance the wind with the water and gravity
relaxed and alert is the only way to be.

In this moment I plainly stand
as ready as I am able to believe that I can
surrender my life willingly into the hands
of my authentic response to Love's master plan.

This is my ride toward freedom on Earth.
I commit to stay with it for all that I'm worth.

Qigong

Digging in the garden all day long.
Lifting the dirt
calling the air
to come infuse *the gong*.

Weeding with my exhales
as faithful as new Love.
Inviting the fierceness of the lion
with the gentleness of the dove.

I make a space for absolute Grace
and feel the Chi answer by lifting my face
to bless and caress and wash clean every trace
of doubt still left growing in me.

It's so sweet
to feel complete
digging in the dirt of my home.
I am tilling and spilling all that I know
to grow what I have not yet been shown.
I dance with the wilderness my heart beat is setting
and enter the moment by releasing regret.

Your sweetness toward me is amending my soil
I fold you right in with handfuls of joy
and watch for the thunder and the beautiful sight
of community in action, of change taking flight.

What will this good day of cultivation yield?

I am aiming for a vision from the unified field.

Oh, My Kinfolk

I come from the land of beginnings with my heart pinned to my sleeve
and I'm bound to sail for Canaan, the home that's promised me.
The rain came down all night that day, I saw what I'd believed
the sky as dry as bone with me determined to be free.
The sun beat down upon my will to try and take my leave
the heat took everything I am and froze my disbelief.

I sing oh, my kinfolk, please do not forsake me;
I have come from the beginning
with my heart pinned to my sleeve.

My night swims with big dreams where I find everything gone still
And in that swirl I see a girl making her way down a hill.
She makes her way down from that hill of thorns and bramble weeds
she comes so close I can't deny that girl I see is me.
The taste of freedom is in her mouth and tears are in her eyes
I hear her say I cannot stay here wearing this disguise.

I sing oh, my sweet kinfolk, please do not mistake me;
I have come from the beginning
with my heart inside my sleeve.

Soon I'll arrive home in my heart with time passed faintly by
I'll look around and see the ground of Truth instead of lies.
And when I find the heart I wear is everything I am
I'll die to all the other things I once believed condemned.
And when I feel the night's too long and I cannot go on
I'll lift my head, accept my death and my God's denouement.

I sing to you who've been my kinfolk, please do not mistake me;
I come from the beginning
with my heart destined to be free.

Sick Of Me

I am sick of this *me* I have made
and I'm sick of the games this *me* plays.
I'm tired of the old it calls new
and these things it insists I must do.

How sick and tired must I be
to surrender this me *and be free?*
How long can I stand to stand by
as the bride of this me's *epic pride?*

All of the effort and strain
to hide behind *me* in my pain
has exhausted *me* and *me's* hope
of surviving outside of what I know.

Now with *me's* hope running dry
along with *me's* reasons to try
there's less cause to restrict my view
to the things my *me* tells me are true.

And so now there's a chance to replace
these thoughts that maintain my disgrace.
In this space *I* stand and *I* wait
for the vision of *I* and the gift of Its grace
refusing everything but
the truth I can feel with my gut.

For possibly the first time in my life
I am trusting that *I* know what's right
And its taking me down to the bone
of all that *me* has called home.
Down past all of the chatter
Down to the heart of what matters.

And the very thing *I* hold most dear
is the last thing that *me* wants to hear.
Still I'm standing here listening hard
as my world is breaking apart
into the splintering shards
of *me's* fearfully misguided guard.

Watching it all through my *I*
I can see a place to stand by
with my heart and my mind open wide
seeing
It was never for *me* to decide.

Don't Forget

Stay awake
 stay awake and take your time.
Don't forget
stay awake
stay right here and remain calm.
Keep your calm by trusting now.
Trust you need not manage how.
Keep in mind you cannot loose
the love you've prayed to God would choose you.
Don't forget
you're sweet and sour and so much more than that besides.
Remember what you're here to do instead of reasons you should hide.
Don't forget
I love you more today than yesterday
and even after time collapses The Way is still The Way.
Trust your heart and take your time
slow your tireless, anxious mind
and let the patterns of fear unwind
exposing perfect truth behind.

Peter Peter pumpkin eater
is a human being human.
So are you
working through
down into the Truth of You.
Don't forget
keep your calm
relax your body and open your mind.
Discover *your* way to stay alert
to the fact Truth can't be hurt.
Most of all
have some fun
while doing your best to remember
We are One.

Published by One Body Books
1711 West 116th Street
Carmel, Indiana USA 46032

Into the Fire: Words Collected on the Road to Silence
Copyright © 2011 by Margaret Coyle.

All rights reserved including the right of reproduction or transmission in whole or part in any form with out prior written permission from Margaret Coyle Irsay. Make inquiries to One Body Books at www.onebodyinc.com

Design:
Susanna Dulkinys
San Francisco, California and Berlin, Germany

Photography:
Tjarn Takuji Sato
California
www.wabishi.com

Printing:
Ruksaldruck
Berlin, Germany

First Edition

Library of Congress
Cataloging-in-Publication
Data Available
ISBN-13: 978-0-9789468-1-4
ISBN-10: 0-9789468-1-2